SIR CHARLES

SIR CHARLES

The Wit and Wisdom of
CHARLES BARKLEY

BY CHARLES BARKLEY
with Rick Reilly

WARNER BOOKS

A Time Warner Company

Editorial Research by Desmond M. Wallace

Warner Books, Inc., 1271 Avenue of the Americas, New York, NY 10020

 A Time Warner Company

Printed in the United States of America
First Printing: April 1994
10 9 8 7 6 5 4 3 2 1

Library of Congress Cataloging-in-Publication Data

Barkley. Charles
   Sir Charles: the wit and wisdom of Charles Barkley / Charles
Barkley with Rick Reilly.
      p. cm.
   ISBN 0-446-51855-7
   1. Barkley, Charles, 1963—Quotations. 2. Barkley, Charles,
1963—Humor. 3. Basketball—United States—Quotations, maxims, etc.
I. Reilly, Rick. II. Title.
GV884.B28A3   1994
796.323'0973—dc20   94-1952
                                                                  CIP

Book design by Leo McRee

O O O

CONTENTS

SIR CHARLES

○ ○ ○

INTRODUCTION

There has never been a Quote King quite like Charles Wade Barkley, the Round Mound of Sound. He has retired the trophy, and all further competition has been canceled.

There have been guys who were louder (Brian "The Boz" Bosworth), guys who went for volume ("Neon" Deion Sanders) and guys who never paused to inhale (Reggie), but nobody has ever handed out the good stuff, the honest, fresh, controversial, funny, smart, can-he-say-that? stuff the way Charles Barkley has.

He has not only been an Olympic gold medal winner, an NBA All-Star eight times, an NBA Most Valuable Player, but been voted NBA All-Interview since his rookie year. No wonder. Your average gravy-stained sportswriters would send a limo to get Barkley to the arena. Barkley gives sportswriters more usable stuff in one western road swing than Kareem did in 22 years. There are some nights when you are sure Barkley is going to drain your Bic of ink, talk the pad right out of paper, exhaust the truck's videotape supply, blow the press run and make SportsCenter run late. Set of routine cuts coming up in training camp? "Harold Katz is afraid to have an all-black team," Barkley says. Boring game in Boston? "As long as [Larry] Bird's around, I'll only be the second-worst defensive player in basketball," Barkley says. Looking for an off-day story on refs? "We don't need refs, but I guess white guys need something to do. All the players are black," says Barkley.

The man makes the job *too* easy. "I believe in expressing what you feel," Barkley once said. "There are people who hide everything inside—and it's guys like that who kill whole families."

Like his gleaming skull, Barkley hides absolutely nothing. And in hiding nothing, he gets in more trouble than redheaded twins. He is perhaps the first modern athlete who simply refuses to take the abuse. If he is being heckled, he will heckle back. If he is being attacked in print, he attacks back with quotes. If he is being harassed, duck.

His game with reporters is a lot like his game on the court. He causes extreme havoc. He is best in dense, sweaty circles. And he always does the dirty work. Michael Jordan once said that Barkley "never holds his tongue. Sometimes he says the things you want to say, but you don't have the courage to say."

Among (a) quantum physics, (b) the infield fly rule and (c) Charles Barkley, the most mis-understood is Barkley, the man America believes eats live chickens for lunch. In truth, Barkley is 99 percent bark, 1 percent bite. Dave Coskey, the longtime Sixer director of public relations once said, "Most of these guys are jerks who want you to think they're nice guys. But Charles is a genuinely nice guy who wants you to think he's a jerk."

In truth, Barkley is as friendly as a school-house dog and as open to the public as a 7-Eleven. For every night your average NBA superstar is staying in his room, Barkley is *out there* swan-diving into people. One night at the Phoenix Suns training camp in Flagstaff, Arizona, Barkley was eating at a local dive across from the hotel. As he tried to eat, fans swamped his table for autographs. Barkley would take a bite, sign, take a bite, sign. One drunk man, slurring his words, kept showing up in line over and over again, rubbing Barkley's famous bald head as he signed, blurting, "I can't believe it's him!" The drunk must have gotten five different autographs and rubbed Barkley's head all five times. Barkley never said a word.

At the Barcelona Olympics, most of the rest of the American Dream Team holed up in its $900-a-night, police-barricaded hotel. Barkley, though, was on his nightly meander through the streets and bars and sidewalk cafés. You'd notice his gleaming head first, then the hundred or so stragglers, gawkers and fans that streamed giddily behind. If the late nights and morning tee times hurt his game, it fooled the world. He was far and away the most outstanding player of the Games.

The world's problem with Barkley comes from a worldwide shortage of sense of humor. "Anybody that takes Charles too seriously," says Phoenix Suns coach Paul Westphal, "needs to get a little more bran in their diets." One afternoon, my family and I ran into him in a hotel lobby. It was still six hours to tip-off. My four-year-old girl looked up at him in awe and said, "Are you Charles Barkley?"

"Yes, I am," he said.

"Are you mean?" she asked.

"Not till 7:30," he said.

—RICK REILLY

○ ○ ○

OPPONENTS

• To Moses Malone, 38, as he walked into the Sun locker room after a game in March 1993: **"The average age in this room just went up 25 years."** —*Arizona Republic,* 3/27/93

○ ○ ○

• On Michael Jordan: **"The black Jesus."** —Denver *Post,* 10/30/93

○ ○ ○

• On the Boston Celtic aging front line of Larry Bird, Robert Parrish and Kevin McHale: **"I'd rather have older guys who are great players than younger guys who stink."** —Los Angeles *Times,* 12/19/90

• On Bill Laimbeer after a scuffle during a game:
"I don't know why he wants to challenge my heavyweight title. He's not even among the top 10 contenders." —New York *Times*, 3/17/91

○ ○ ○

• On being fined $22,000 after a fight with Bill Laimbeer, plus $31,700 in suspended salary:
"I don't care if I get fined. I make $3 million. What's a couple thousand dollars?"
—*Sports Illustrated*, 4/30/90

○ ○ ○

• On Larry Bird:
"As long as Bird's around, I'll only be the second-worst defensive player in basketball."
—New York *Times*, 3/17/91

○ ○ ○

• On the possibility of Bird guarding him one-on-one:
"They [the Celtics] would never dare guard us man for man. That would be a dream come true, for their 3-man [small forward] to guard me. Having Larry guard me would be my wildest dream." —Boston *Globe*, 3/29/90

• On which players impressed him after a Phoenix exhibition game in Europe:
"No. 5, No. 11, No. 14."

—Denver *Post*, 11/1/93

○ ○ ○

• On then-Washington Bullet center Moses Malone, who had vowed to remain silent until the Bullets reached the .500 mark:
"I guess he won't be talking for a few years."

—Los Angeles *Times*, 3/25/88

○ ○ ○

• On Kevin McHale and the Celtics:
"Kevin McHale is the best player I ever played against. Bar none. You had to hope he was missing. You couldn't stop him. In his prime he was the best. He was too big for me and everybody on him, whether it was Moses [Malone] or Bobby Jones. That Celtics front line was the greatest front line ever to play the game. There were no weaknesses."

—*Playboy*, 5/93

• On comparisons to Michael Jordan:

"I would *never* say another player is better than me. *Never.* I'm not going to say I'm better than him but I would never say he's better than me 'cause I can play basketball with any basketball player in this world."

—NBC, 6/16/93

(Game 4 interview with Bob Costas)

○ ○ ○

• On player management:

"In Philly, Armon Gilliam used to say the only reason I was better than him was because I got the ball more. I said, 'I get the ball more because you ain't worth a dime.' In Phoenix, they ain't jealous of me. And the same in New York. Patrick [Ewing] is the man, and the others reap the benefits. They're not knuckleheads. That's how New York got good; they got rid of the knuckleheads."

—New York *Times,* 5/27/93

○ ○ ○

• On Mark Price:

"He's the best point guard in the NBA today. He's a weapon. He's a great scorer and knows how to run a team. He may not get the kind of publicity he deserves, but he gets the publicity from the players. That's all that matters."

—Cleveland *Plain Dealer,* 3/2/93

• On a flagrant foul committed against the Denver Nugget Scott Hastings:
"I've still got a problem with him from the Philly-Detroit game three years ago. He sucker-punched me. He and I do not get along. I'll get him someday, and I don't want anybody breaking it up when I do."
—*Arizona Republic*, 4/10/93

○ ○ ○

• On Michael Jordan's golf:
"If he's playing as hard as all these books say he's playing, I must be the only one he's better than." —*The Charlie Rose Show*, 12/3/93

○ ○ ○

• On Chuck Person:
"Get me the ball and let me torture him."
—*New York Times*, 3/17/91

○ ○ ○

• On shoving a scrawny Angolan basketball player during an Olympic game in Barcelona:
"It's a ghetto thing. You wouldn't understand." —*Boston Globe*, 8/9/92

• More on elbowing the skinny Angolan player:
"**I'll hit a fat guy next time.**"
> —St. Louis *Post-Dispatch*, 7/29/92

○ ○ ○

• On Brazilian star Oscar Schmidt:
"**Isn't he that guy with Felix Unger?**"
> —Philadelphia *Inquirer*, 7/23/92

○ ○ ○

• On whom he'd like to play with:
"**I wouldn't mind playing with Patrick Ewing and Charles Oakley. I'd kill to have someone on my team fight me for a rebound.**"
> —Washington *Post*, 5/13/91

○ ○ ○

• On the New York Knicks:
"**I love the Knicks' style because they beat each other up. You got to be a man to play with them boys. Intimidation. It's like Nolan Ryan and Ronnie Lott. You get too close to the plate and Ryan throws at your head to back you off. Same thing with the Knicks. Do I like that? I like playing any game when a man plays. Boys stay home.**"
> —New York *Times*, 5/27/93

• On Cuba, the Dream Team's first opponent in the Tournament of the Americas:

"All I know is that they're led by some old scruffy guy with a beard who smokes cigars."

—Detroit *News,* 7/3/92

○ ○ ○

• On the Dream Team's goal against Panama in the Tournament of the Americas:

"To get the Canal back."

—Detroit *News,* 7/3/92

○ ○ ○

• On the NBA's future:

"There will be another Michael Jordan, another Larry Bird, and another Charles Barkley. God is so good to us. If someone told you five years ago a 6-foot-4, 250-pound guy would lead the league in rebounding, you'd say I was full of shit. If someone told you there'd be a 6-foot-10 guy from Nigeria, Hakeem Olajuwon, who could outrun guards, you wouldn't believe it. If someone told you there'd be a white guy 5-foot-whatever who could play like John Stockton, you wouldn't believe that either. They just keep coming." —Boston *Globe,* 2/19/89

• On hatred of opponents:
"I don't hate anyone, at least not for more than 48 minutes, barring overtime."

—*Outrageous,* p. 206

O O O

○ ○ ○

PLACES

• On the city of Phoenix:
"This is the only place in the world where Michael Jackson isn't as popular as Garth Brooks." —*Arizona Republic,* 6/25/93

○ ○ ○

• On playing sports in Phoenix:
"If you want to get your ass beat, get it beat in the sun. At least if you lose here you can play golf and let your frustrations go." —*Arizona Republic,* 6/25/93

○ ○ ○

• On not being able to find the 1993 World Series on TV in Germany:
"It shouldn't be called the World Series if everybody can't watch it. Maybe they should call it the Almost World Series."

—Associated Press, 10/21/93

○ ○ ○

• On his popularity in Japan, where his Nike commercial with Godzilla was being aired:
"Godzilla is big over there. Very, very big. In fact, Godzilla is bigger than Michael Jordan in Japan. Hey, the Japanese think Nike is a Greek god. And, yeah, I think they're right. Nike is a Greek god."   —*Arizona Republic,* 3/1/93

○ ○ ○

• On midwestern cities:
"I hate those places. They roll up the sidewalks at 10 o'clock every night, which means that there are no decent restaurants open by the time the team leaves the arena. And after games NBA players are like hungry animals on the prowl—always for food and often for companionship, too."   —*Outrageous,* p. 160

• Asked at the 1992 Barcelona Olympics if he missed the U.S.:
"I miss the crime and murder. I haven't heard about any good shootings or stabbings lately. There haven't been any brutal stabbings or anything in the last 24 hours. I really miss it."
—Boston *Globe,* 8/9/92

○ ○ ○

• On participating in the 1990 NBA All-Star game in Miami despite a pulled groin:
"It would have been nice to sit in Philadelphia freezing and relaxing. I guess I have to suffer here in Florida and play with Michael Jordan, Isiah Thomas, and Patrick Ewing. I'll make the best of it."
—*Newsday,* 2/11/90

○ ○ ○

• On coming home after an 11-day, six-game East Coast road trip:
"Real glad to be back. You pay as much for a house as I did, you might as well spend time in it." —*Arizona Republic,* 1/30/93

○ ○ ○

• On an October 1993 trip to Munich for the McDonald's Open, Barkley was asked by a relatively short reporter to assess the gap between European basketball and the NBA:
"About your height to my height."
—Associated Press, 10/21/93

○ ○ ○

• To a Lithuanian interpreter who was translating a conversation with star forward Rimas Kurtinaitis during the 1989 NBA All-Star Weekend:
"Think he'd like to go out to a strip joint?"
—Washington *Post,* 2/12/89

○ ○ ○

• On whether geography was a tough course at his alma mater, Auburn:
"Never realized which class was difficult and which one was easy. As long as I was leading the SEC in rebounding, I was getting a passing grade." —Arizona *Republic,* 3/20/93

○ ○ ○

• On New York:
"I love New York City. I've got a gun."
—*Newsday,* 3/13/91

• On what he likes about Arizona:
"We've got to change the laws. . . . I'm just telling you all, the left-hand lane is for speeders. Not for people who are going to drive the speed limit. Remember that, Arizonans. That's the only problem I got with the state so far. People have a tendency to drive in the left-hand lane, driving the speed limit."

—*Arizona Republic,* 6/25/93

• When a cockroach moved by Barkley's feet in the Suns locker room at Chicago Stadium during the NBA finals:
"Damn, I'm back in Alabama!"

—*Arizona Republic,* 9/26/93

○ ○ ○

REFS

• "I don't listen to the refs. I don't listen to anyone who makes less money than I do."
—*USA Today*, 5/26/93

○ ○ ○

• Complaining to referee Darell Garretson after he thought he was fouled during a game in San Antonio:
"I know women who don't hold me that tight."
—*Arizona Republic*, 6/25/93

○ ○ ○

• Complaining to NBA referee Tommy Nunez that the other two officials were missing calls: **"Tommy, you've got to make that call. You know Moe and Larry won't."**

—*Sporting News*, 3/26/90

○ ○ ○

• On being thrown out of a game by referee Bob Delaney for throwing elbows at guard John Bagley in a game against the New Jersey Nets:
"There was a fly on my arm and I had an itch in my armpit and I was trying to get rid of both, and I moved my arms. He didn't even give me a chance to explain."

—*New York Times*, 2/15/88

○ ○ ○

• On veteran referee Mike Mathis:
"I hate him and he hates me."

—*Playboy*, 5/93

○ ○ ○

• **"We don't need refs, but I guess white guys need something to do. All the players are black."**

—*Sporting News*, 3/26/90

• On whether his comic book, *Charles Barkley and the Referee Murders*, was a onetime publication:

"No, it's a series. There's a lot of referees to kill."   —*Arizona Republic*, 10/12/93

○ ○ ○

FANS

• "I think anybody who charges for an autograph is an asshole. I don't know who's the bigger asshole, the guy who pays for it or the one who sells it."

—Knight-Ridder, 1/9/91

○ ○ ○

• On Boston fans:
"I don't like the people of Boston. I think I should call Ripley's because they have the greatest collection of assholes ever up here [Boston]. The crowd doesn't bother me. I'm glad they came. They paid a couple guys' salaries."　　　　　—Sporting News, 12/15/86

• On why, despite his tough-guy image, people like him:

"People respect honesty. There are a lot of athletes out there who are just walking P.R. firms." —NBC, 6/16/93

(Game 4 interview with Bob Costas)

○ ○ ○

• To a heckler who said that Barkley would never get a championship ring:

"Yeah, but I've got $20 million."

—Associated Press, 6/19/92

○ ○ ○

• On controversy:

"I got a reputation for being controversial. I resent that. I am one of the few athletes in the world who is for real. I'm not phony. Fans respect me for giving my all and showing emotion." —Knight-Ridder, 1/9/91

○ ○ ○

• On Milwaukee fans after a 1988 Eastern Conference semifinal game:

"These fans can kiss me where the sun don't shine. They're not here to cheer their team. They're here to harass."

—Philadelphia *Daily News,* 5/8/86

• "I try to keep my distance from the fans. If they can turn on a guy who helped us get to the NBA finals [Suns point guard Kevin Johnson] . . . it makes me wonder, if I struggle, would they do the same thing to me?"

—NBC, 6/16/93
(Game 4 interview with Bob Costas)

• After receiving a box of chocolate chip cookies from an anonymous fan:
"Naw, give it away, just in case it's got poison or something in it. Might be from a Pistons fan." —Knight-Ridder, 1/9/91

• On popularity:
"I don't care if people like me. They don't know nothing just like the media. They can't bother me. I'm getting paid for the next 80 years." —Los Angeles Times, 2/22/87

• On Philadelphia fans and the possibility of moving the team across the Delaware River to Camden, New Jersey:
"I'm serious. I think if we move to south Jersey people will appreciate it more. Guys want to play in front of big crowds. It really doesn't bother me. I'm going to get paid regardless of who comes."   —New York *Times*, 2/14/90

○ ○ ○

• "I have one basic rule: I treat the person how they treat me, whether that's good or bad. I'm a nice guy but I don't mind being a jerk."
—Los Angeles *Times*, 2/22/87

○ ○ ○

• On the lack of fan support in Philadelphia:
"I love Philadelphia. I love playing in front of 8,000 fans every night."
—Sporting *News*, 3/26/90

○ ○ ○

• On a shouting match with a fan during the 1993 Western Conference championship:
"For me to do something obscene, somebody has to be doing something to me that's really

obscene. I don't go to a game and say that I'm going to make an obscene gesture to a fan. Something has to provoke me."

—NBC, 6/16/93
(Game 4 interview with Bob Costas)

• When asked if he wanted to attend any of the inaugural balls in Washington in January 1993: "No, those are not my type of people. I like being around low-class people. Reporters."

—Minneapolis *Star Tribune*, 1/27/93

○ ○ ○
RACE

• On the 1990s coverage of him by Philadelphia's two daily papers:
"I'm a '90s nigger. The *Daily News* and the *Inquirer* have been on my back. Everything I do is wrong. They want their black athletes to be Uncle Toms. I told you white boys you've never heard of a '90s nigger. We do what we want to do." —Associated Press, 6/19/92

○ ○ ○

• On why blacks excel at basketball:
"It doesn't cost anything to play."
—Cleveland *Plain Dealer*, 3/2/93

• On Cincinnati Red owner Marge Schott:
"Marge Schott can say 'money-grubbing Jew' or 'million-dollar niggers' because that's the society we live in. People say it's freedom of speech. That's not freedom of speech. . . . The worst thing is that she may go kiss up to them [blacks]. When the Reds won the World Series, she was drinking champagne with the brothers and calling them million-dollar niggers behind their backs. I have more respect for the Klan, because when they call you nigger they don't sit there and drink with you."

—*Playboy*, 5/93

• "Things haven't gotten better 'cause we, as Black America, are getting worse and we as athletes . . . the money's not funneling down to Black America. I'm not going to begrudge White America. But we actually help White America more than we help Black America 'cause they're paying us but making more off of us."

—*Up Close with Roy Firestone*, ESPN, 2/7/93

• On double standards in America:
"There's a double standard for blacks and whites. That's it. But there's this thing: if you're a black athlete you're going to have to watch yourself a little more closely.... The media has this thing where we like black athletes as long as they stay in their place and make us money and do as we tell them. Well, that's not right.... My thing is if I'm good enough to make the money, I'm good enough to voice my opinion."
    —*Up Close with Roy Firestone*, ESPN, 2/7/93

○ ○ ○

• "When you're a kid, you don't think racist. When you grow up, that's when you become racist. Some knucklehead teaches you to be racist.... There are black people I don't want to be around, and there are white people I don't want to be around."
                    —*Playboy*, 5/93

○ ○ ○

• On wanting to be a member at an all-white country club:
"There are a lot of exclusionary practices at these golf courses as far as blacks are concerned. I don't know what they think we're going to do. I guess they think we're going to

walk around with a big jukebox, bring all the boys, play in the hedges. . . . I love golf. It's my favorite sport. And just because I'm black I can play places, but I can't join and that's not right."

—*Up Close with Roy Firestone*, ESPN, 2/7/93

○ ○ ○

• "Life is not all about scoring 20 points and 10 boards a game. But that's all they ask me about. Racism is something we should be discussing. But people are tired of hearing about that. Nobody talks about the homeless, or the budget, or the obligation we have to the kids in this country. People like to believe the world begins and ends with basketball. Well, it doesn't." —Boston *Globe*, 1/17/92

○ ○ ○

• Recalling a conversation with Phoenix Suns V.P. Cotton Fitzsimmons, an admitted Republican, about the 1992 presidential election:

"I told him I was a Bill Clinton man and a black millionaire. He said if Clinton got elected, I'd just be black."

—*Sports Illustrated*, 5/3/93

• "People say that I'm in the NBA and getting paid so I should shut up. I'll never do that. If I only tried to do the right thing and say the right thing I'd lose my soul. I won't be their Uncle Tom and just go along with the program."   —Washington *Post,* 11/17/91

O O O

• "Anytime you're a black person with a strong personality, it turns society against you."
                    —*USA Today,* 8/3/92

O O O

• On his belief that the Sixers kept Dave Hoppen, the only white player on the Sixers one year, because of his skin color:
"I don't think Harold [owner Harold Katz] is racist, but it would surprise me if we had an all-black team, and I'll stick by that. There's a certain minority of people out there who are racist, who don't want to see an all-black team and would complain. [Katz] has to think about his ticket-buyers."
                —Washington *Times,* 10/31/91

O O O

• "You know, the brothers can't go to medical school or law school. They can't be presidents of corporations, but they sure do like to play basketball."

—Minneapolis *Star Tribune,* 6/28/92

• "One of my problems is I scare people. I'm big and I'm black. A strong man who is black. That's double scary."

—Boston *Globe,* 1/17/92

• "Michael Jordan, Eddie Murphy, Arsenio Hall, these people are not treated the same as other blacks in society. You might listen to black music and you might watch black athletes, but that doesn't mean you'll be willing to talk to that black guy who just moved down the street."   —Boston *Globe,* 1/17/92

○ ○ ○
FAME

• On personality:
"I don't want to be like everybody else. . . .
Nobody wants to shoot in the last two or three
minutes of a game. I do. Somebody has to be
the hero. It might as well be me."

—*Playboy*, 5/93

• On the double-edged sword of celebrity:
"When you're the top dog, everybody wants to
put you in the pound."

—Los Angeles *Times*, 3/24/93

• On pressure he feels being a star player on a team:

"Pressure is when I get to the Pearly Gates and God says to me, 'Oops, sorry, you're going to hell.'" —*Arizona Republic,* 6/25/93

○ ○ ○

• On why his new line of basketball shoes, Nike Air Max, wasn't named after him:

"So that people who hate me will still buy them. It might help indirectly, if my name isn't on them." —*Arizona Republic,* 4/12/93

○ ○ ○

• On his Rose Bowl tickets:

"They're at the 50-yard line. Where else? I'm a star." —*Arizona Republic,* 1/30/93

○ ○ ○

• On being harassed by fans:

"Just because we're in the limelight, we shouldn't have to take a lot of crap off people." —New York *Daily News,* 1/24/92

○ ○ ○

HOOPS

• After watching from the bench in street clothes because of a shoulder injury at a Suns-Minnesota Timberwolves game:
"Are the games this boring when I'm playing?"
—*Arizona Republic*, 4/15/93

• Upon hearing that he had been traded from the Philadelphia 76ers to the Phoenix Suns:
"Phoenix is not a bad place. I could play golf every day."
—Associated Press, 6/18/92

• On the NBA's reaction (and $5,000 fine) to his bet with Mark Jackson during the 1989–90 season on who would take the last shot of the game:

"I went to bed as Charlie Barkley and woke up as Pete Rose."   —Boston *Globe,* 1/21/90

○ ○ ○

• On retirement:

"Like Larry Bird said, it's time for someone else to be the hero."   —Denver *Post,* 11/28/93

○ ○ ○

• On the lack of defense at NBA All-Star games:

"I don't play much defense for the Phoenix Suns either. I get paid to score and rebound. I'll need another $1 million for defense."

—*Arizona Republic,* 6/25/93

○ ○ ○

• **"You can't compare preseason to regular season. Preseason is just a way to screw fans out of money."**

—*Sports Illustrated,* 11/30/92

○ ○ ○

• On shooting:
"The only difference between a good shot and a bad shot is if it goes in or not."
  —*Up Close with Roy Firestone,* ESPN, 2/7/93

○ ○ ○

• On why the Suns traded Tim Perry:
"They had to trade Tim Perry. He's number 34."   —Los Angeles *Times,* 6/21/92

○ ○ ○

• On why he wore number 23 and not his own number 34 at the All-Star game in Salt Lake City:
"That [23] was [Suns owner] Jerry Colangelo's number at Illinois. Wearing it was my way of thanking him for taking me out of purgatory."
            —Cleveland *Plain Dealer,* 3/2/93

○ ○ ○

• On rebounding from a regular season loss to the Bulls to beat the Portland Trail Blazers:
"NBA stands for No Babies Allowed."
            —*Arizona Republic,* 6/25/93

○ ○ ○

• On the difference between college and the pros:
"[In the NBA] a season is like a marathon, a test of endurance, of your manhood. It's not like college. Anyone can win the NCAA's but when you win the NBA, you've done something. A hundred games. That ain't easy. College, you just got to upset someone one time and you can play zone and all that happy camper stuff. But here in the pros the best team wins."   —New York Times, 5/27/93

O O O

• On the new 76er uniforms:
"They look like my daughter got a hold of some crayons."   —Associated Press, 6/19/92

O O O

• On scoring:
"I don't want to lead the league in scoring. Any idiot can score. All you have to do is shoot a lot. The only individual statistics I really care about are rebounds and assists."
—USA Today, 12/21/90

O O O

• On physical play:
"When a guy comes down the lane, I want him to be wondering what side I'm going to hit him from." —*The Charlie Rose Show,* 12/3/93

O O O

• Barkley T-shirt sold at AmericaWest Arena in Phoenix:
"All Bark and All Bite."
—Los Angeles *Times,* 6/24/92

O O O

• On what he expects from Michael Jordan's retirement:
"The only good thing about Michael retiring is that he's going to have to give me some strokes the next time we play golf. His handicap is going to go way down this year, I know that."
—*Arizona Republic,* 10/16/93

O O O

• On pressure: **"Pressure is for tires."**
—*Sports Illustrated,* 11/9/92

O O O

• Barkley to Western Conference rival and Utah Jazz forward Karl Malone after the newest Sun learned of his trade from the Sixers:

"There's a new sheriff in the West. Gonna be some changes 'round these parts."

—*Sports Illustrated,* 11/9/92

○ ○ ○

• On what would have happened if his former team, the Sixers, had drafted Brad Daugherty and not traded his rights to the Cavaliers in 1986:

"I can't answer that for sure, but let's put it like this: . . . With a front line of me, Daugherty and Moses [Malone], we'd have had a couple of championship rings by now. Who would have stopped us?"

—Cleveland *Plain Dealer,* 3/2/93

○ ○ ○

• On attitude:

"I don't have a bad temper except during games." —*The National,* 4/25/91

○ ○ ○

• On pro basketball players in the Olympics:
"Other teams have been sending their pros for years. Now they can take their whipping and go home." —*Arizona Republic,* 6/20/92

○ ○ ○

• On being late to a January 19, 1987, Philadelphia 76er pregame meeting before a game against the Phoenix Suns:
"These games interfere with my soap operas." —random unlabeled clip

○ ○ ○

• On why he couldn't have played again for the 76ers:
"Suppose your wife says that she's been shopping around all summer looking for a better husband, but would take you back if she couldn't find one."
—Los Angeles *Times,* 7/11/92

○ ○ ○

• On his rugged playing style:
"[NBA V.P. of operations] Rod Thorn said, 'Don't hurt anybody.' He didn't say, 'Don't hit anybody.' " —New York *Times,* 6/18/90

• On putting his job in perspective:
"Basketball is just my job. It's not that important in the scheme of things."

—New York *Times,* 6/19/93

○ ○ ○

• On how he views being traded, from a Philadelphia perspective:
"I thought they'd be a lot better. I figured [Jeff] Hornacek, [Andrew] Lang and [Tim] Perry would make them pretty good. I guess they should have gotten Shaquille [O'Neal], Kareem [Abdul–Jabbar] and Magic [Johnson] to make that team better."

—Cleveland *Plain Dealer,* 3/2/93

○ ○ ○

• On winning the 1993 NBA MVP Award:
"I can't explain the last year of my life. Nobody gets it this good."

—*Arizona Republic,* 6/25/93

○ ○ ○

○ ○ ○

KIDS

• "Kids are great. That's one of the best things about our business, all the kids you get to meet. It's a shame that they have to grow up and be regular people and come to games and call you names." —Los Angeles *Times,* 7/6/91

○ ○ ○

• To a six-year-old fan after he told Barkley that he wanted to be like the then-Sixer star forward:
"Naaaaw, you want to be like Donald Trump because he gets the best babes."
—Washington *Post,* 2/27/91

• "I don't believe athletes should be role models. I believe parents should be role models. . . . It's not like when I was growing up. My mom and my grandmother told me how it was going to be. If I didn't like it, they said, 'Don't let the door hit you in the ass on your way out.' "

—*Arizona Republic*, 6/25/93

• On endorsements:
"I have a sneaker deal myself, but I don't understand why people would buy one sneaker endorsed by one player over the other. Kids idolize professional athletes, which is wrong in itself. . . . To kids that idolize me, I tell them don't do it just because I can dribble a basketball—that's really sick."   —*People*, 2/5/90

• On having rats in the house as a kid growing up in Leeds, Alabama:
"Yeah, there were a few. But I don't have to worry about that anymore 'cause I can afford an exterminator—and a new house."

—*Up Close with Roy Firestone*, ESPN, 2/7/93

• On being a role model:
"If the only qualification for being a role model is that you have to be able to dunk a basketball, then I know millions of people who could become role models. That's not enough. Hell, I know drug dealers who can dunk. So, can drug dealers be role models, too?"   —Associated Press, 6/19/92

○ ○ ○

• On society:
"We screwed our kids up. We've taught them that the only way you can be successful is if you make a lot of money. And now we're complaining because they're killing each other for jewelry and drugs and money. Now we're trying to stop it in midstream."
                —*The Charlie Rose Show,* 12/3/93

○ ○ ○

• "I wish every kid could be me, but they can't. They need to get an education, get a job. People look at this life as money, cars, being on TV every day. You know, I just didn't wake up being Charles Barkley. There's a lot of work that goes into it."
                —*Arizona Republic,* 5/29/93

• From a Nike shoe commercial:

"This is my new shoe. It's a good shoe. It won't make you dunk like me. It won't make you rich like me. It won't make you rebound like me. It definitely won't make you handsome like me. It'll only make you have shoes like me. Period."

—*The Charlie Rose Show,* 12/3/93

○ ○ ○

• On role models:

"If these kids are half as successful as me, they'll be fine."   —NBC, 6/16/93

(Game 4 interview with Bob Costas)

○ ○ ○

○ ○ ○
SELF

• "Can't nobody on planet Earth guard me. No one. I mean that." —New York *Times*, 3/17/91

○ ○ ○

• On his relative lack of height given his extra-ordinary rebounding ability:
"If I were 7 feet tall, I'd be illegal in three states." —Knight-Ridder, 2/15/89

○ ○ ○

• "Sometimes when I do things it just happens. It sounds like a cliché. I think God is in my body." —Washington *Post*, 5/2/90

• "God gave a lot of players in the NBA talent. I don't want to be like them. I want to be a step above."

—Roy Firestone, *Mouths That Roared*, p. 69

○ ○ ○

• "I don't think I'm better than anybody unless I'm on the court."

—Los Angeles *Times*, 2/22/87

○ ○ ○

• "Height is overrated. I've played with a lot of big stiffs."

—*The Charlie Rose Show*, 12/3/93

○ ○ ○

• "God just made me special and that's the only way you can look at it. There will never be another 6'4" guy who can accomplish what I've accomplished. Ever. Ever."

—New York *Times*, 3/17/91

○ ○ ○

• "I know I'm one of the best players in the league. I can play with anybody. I don't need the MVP to tell me that."

—*Sporting News*, 2/22/88

• On a game against Seattle in which he thought he'd played poorly yet had 19 points, 13 rebounds and nine assists:

"I can't believe it. I amaze myself. How many guys can play like that and almost have a triple double? About two, that's how many. Me and Michael Jordan."

—*Sporting News,* 3/11/91

○ ○ ○

• On his eating habits:

"People say I eat a lot. I really don't. More or less I just eat all the time."

—New York *Times,* 4/24/84

○ ○ ○

• On his image:

"Sooner or later, I'll probably get what I deserve. I'll probably be dead and gone, but people will say, 'That mother was awesome.' "

—Salt Lake City *Tribune,* 2/17/91

○ ○ ○

• "You got to believe in yourself. Hell, I believe I'm the best-looking guy in the world. And I might be right."

—*Arizona Republic,* 6/25/93

• "There's only a few guys great enough so they don't really have any special position: Magic, Michael Jordan, and me."

—*Village Voice*, 6/6/89

O O O

• On preparing for games:
"Practice to me is irrelevant. Just play the game, baby." —*USA Today*, 10/22/93

O O O

• "Anytime I'm on a team, we've got a chance to win." —Philadelphia *Daily News*, 4/25/91

O O O

• On the possibility of being traded:
"I don't think about getting traded. I don't worry about getting traded. If they trade me, somebody is gonna get a helluva player. And that's just a fact. . . . And if I go somewhere, that team automatically is gonna be better."

—Philadelphia *Daily News*, 4/25/91

O O O

• On his contribution to the Sixers:
"There's one reason why the team's been competitive the last six years. The last three or four years—especially with the trades that we've made—there's one reason we've been respectable. You figure it out."
—Salt Lake City *Tribune*, 2/17/91

○ ○ ○

• On his affection for his mother:
"If loving and respecting your mother and being proud of her makes you a mama's boy, then that's what I am."   —*USA Today*, 2/9/90

○ ○ ○

• "Do I lose confidence? Never. That's what separates good players from bad players. Learned that from Andrew Toney."
—New York *Times*, 6/25/93

○ ○ ○

• When asked what his playing weight was:
"Whatever I am when it's time to play, that's my playing weight."
—Los Angeles *Times*, 2/22/87

• "I'm paid to kick ass on the basketball court." —*The National*, 4/25/91

○ ○ ○

• "I'm one of my favorite people."
—*Playboy*, 5/93

○ ○ ○

• After a Game 3 triple-overtime win over the Chicago Bulls in the 1993 NBA finals:
"Can't nobody say shit about our intensity and heart." —*TNT Sports*, 6/13/93

○ ○ ○

• On Chicago police, which had boarded up windows of storefronts before Game 5 of the finals, fearing rioting in the wake of a Bulls win, a win that never came about:
"Take down the plywood, Chicago. There ain't going to be no rioting tonight."
—NBC, interview after game, 6/18/93

○ ○ ○

• After a 1990 brawl between the Sixers and the Pistons:
"I won two titles tonight. I won the division title with my teammates, and I retained my undisputed heavyweight championship of the world."

—Sporting News, 5/7/90

• "There will never be another player like me. I'm the ninth wonder of the world."

—Minneapolis *Star Tribune,* 1/27/93

○ ○ ○

OTHERS

• Frank Layden, former Utah Jazz head coach: "Sigmund Freud would jump out of the grave to examine Charles Barkley."

—*The National,* 4/25/91

○ ○ ○

• Derek Smith, former Sixer forward: "The thing about Charles is that he's his biggest fan. Charles Barkley is a bigger fan of Charles Barkley than any person in the world." —*Sporting News,* 3/25/90

○ ○ ○

• Michael Jordan, on Barkley's frankness:
"He never holds his tongue. Sometimes he says the things you want to say, but you don't have the courage to say."
—*New York Times Magazine,* 3/17/92

○ ○ ○

• Former Sixer teammate Rick Mahorn:
"To play with him you can't sit back and be in awe of him, but you can also sit back and appreciate that he's playing with you instead of against you."   —Washington *Post,* 5/2/90

○ ○ ○

• A Philadelphia writer after being asked if he had seen evidence of a more mature Charles Barkley:
"You mean aside from the 26 technicals, five ejections and $32,000 in fines?"
—Los Angeles *Times,* 5/8/90

○ ○ ○

• Orlando general manager Pat Williams on the early-NBA Barkley:
"He's so fat his bathtub has stretch marks."
—*Sporting News,* 1/21/92

○ ○ ○

• Barney, the impossibly cheerful dinosaur of children's TV, after going one on one with Barkley during Barkley's September 25 stint as guest host of *Saturday Night Live*, a battle that left his tail bent and one eyeball dangling from its socket:
"Charles told me I'm special."
                    —*Sports Illustrated*, 12/27/93

○ ○ ○

• Paul Westphal on Barkley being honored as Mr. Arizona Chamber of Commerce:
"Was that the same guy people said would never fit in here? The next thing you know is he'll be kissing babies down at City Hall."
                    —*Arizona Republic*, 4/15/93

○ ○ ○

• Boston Celtics coach Chris Ford:
"I love Charles because he's so honest. You can see a thought form in his head and then move right out his mouth without stopping in between."   —Los Angeles *Times*, 6/19/91

○ ○ ○

• Orlando *Sentinel* columnist Brian Schmitz on Barkley's plan to deduct $4,500 in fines from his income tax:
"I can see Charles putting Bill Laimbeer in a headlock and saying, 'Hey, it's a business expense.'"   —Los Angeles *Times,* 8/4/90

○ ○ ○

• Philadelphia *Daily News* columnist Bill Conlon on Barkley being traded to Phoenix:
"The needle on the Fun Meter now rests on zero."   —Philadelphia *Daily News,* 6/18/92

○ ○ ○

• Philadelphia *Inquirer* writer Bill Lyon:
"Has Philadelphia ever had a more enchanting, exasperating, confounding, inspiring, combustible, caring and controversial mercenary than Charles Wade Barkley? In a word, no."
      —Philadelphia *Inquirer,* 6/18/92

○ ○ ○

• Paul Westphal on Barkley's 21-point, nine-rebound, seven-assist, three-steal game one night:
"Charles gets you 15 rebounds and 25 points every night and sometimes he has a good game."   —Minneapolis *Star Tribune,* 1/27/93

• Former Philadelphia general manager (and current Washington Bullets G.M.) John Nash:
"Ninety-nine percent of Charles Barkley is good. The other one percent you might want to change. But if you did, who knows how it would affect the 99 percent? What we have come to say in Philadelphia is that when you get Charles Barkley, you get the whole package."   —*Sporting News,* 3/26/90

○ ○ ○

• Pat Williams, general manager of the Orlando Magic:
"Charles once told me he would write his autobiography as soon as he could figure out who the main character would be."
     —Glenn Liebman, *Sports Shorts,* 1993

○ ○ ○

• Former Sixer P.R. director Dave Coskey on Barkley being his first child's godfather:
"My late grandmother, bless her heart, questioned why I would let a black man be my son's godfather. But if there's anybody who I want my child to emulate, it's Charles Barkley. But that's with an asterisk: Charles Barkley off the court." —Knight-Ridder, 1/9/91

• NBC basketball announcer Marv Albert:
"When I step back, a lot of things he says make sense. I think he's the best interview of any professional athlete."
—New York *Daily News,* 1/24/92

O O O

• Paul Westphal:
"Only one person gets to be Elvis. And only one person gets to be Charles Barkley. That's why we got him."   —Mesa *Tribune,* 6/18/92

O O O

○ ○ ○

TEAM

• On the advantages of playing alongside 255-pound Rick Mahorn in Philadelphia:

"It means people will be able to see I don't have the biggest butt in the league."

—*Sports Illustrated*, 11/27/89

○ ○ ○

• On why he shouldn't be criticized for not making the Sixers better:

"That's bull. Me and Michael Jordan always get a bad rap. All you ever hear is that Magic [Johnson] and Larry [Bird] are the only ones who make anybody else better. My thing is, who is it easier to make better—[James] Worthy, [Kevin] McHale or Jayson Williams?"

—*Sporting News*, 1/28/91

• On waiting for former Los Angeles Laker A. C. Green to decide whether to accept the Phoenix Suns free-agent offer:

"He's waiting for God to lead him the right way. I told him I've talked to God, too. He said he was a Suns fan."

—New York Times, 9/27/93

O O O

• To Sixer teammates who happened to be shooting around before a game against the Rockets in 1992:

"What are you doing shooting before a game? If you don't know it by now, it's too late."

—Houston Chronicle, 2/21/92

O O O

• On then-teammate Moses Malone:

"Having him around means there's somebody uglier than me on the team."

—Los Angeles Times, 12/14/84

O O O

• On the most influential person in his basketball life:

"Obviously, Moses [Malone] was the most influential person in my basketball career.

Moses taught me not to trust anybody, to work hard, not to worry about hype, the fans, the media. He said to be my own man because nobody else will be there when push came to shove. I call Moses 'Dad.' "
—New York *Times*, 5/25/93

○ ○ ○

• On the Phoenix Cardinals:
"There's only one team in town and that's the Phoenix Suns. No, I'm not a Cardinals fan. They remind me of the 76ers. Both just put a team out there to make money. They can do it because of revenue sharing and television. But that don't make it right. You owe it to the fans to put a good team out there."
—Cleveland *Plain Dealer*, 3/1/93

○ ○ ○

• On why he didn't take new teammate Oliver Miller along with him to play golf earlier this year:
"The course I went to wouldn't allow more than one black."
—Cleveland *Plain Dealer*, 3/2/93

• On Miller, who helped Barkley shave his head before the preseason Suns game against the Golden State Warriors:

"Oliver really can't play. He's just here to cut my hair. We drafted him out of Arkansas two years ago as our team barber."

—*Arizona Republic,* 10/16/93

○ ○ ○

• On then-teammate 7'7" Manute Bol:

"And I thought I had trouble finding pants that fit." —*Sports Illustrated,* 12/17/90

○ ○ ○

• On Bol:

"He's a one-dimensional player who doesn't give you anything except blocked shots . . . we traded a first-round draft choice for a 28-year-old flyswatter who could score only 1.9 points a game. Hell, my grandmother could score two points a game, as long as she wasn't double-teamed." —*Outrageous,* p. 197

○ ○ ○

• On Rick Mahorn's decision to leave Europe to play for the Sixers:

"Rick may be ugly but he ain't stupid. He was on the next flight." —*Outrageous,* p. 261

• A letter to Bill Laimbeer during the 1989–90 season:
"Dear Bill, Fuck you. Love, Charles Barkley."
—*Outrageous*, p. 203

○ ○ ○

• On why people call him and Mahorn "Bump and Thump":
"I bump 'em and Rick thumps 'em."
—*New York Times Magazine*, 3/17/91

○ ○ ○

• On Detroit Piston point guard Isiah Thomas:
"Isiah will cut your balls off in order to win."
—*Outrageous*, p. 203

○ ○ ○

• After a preseason game against the Detroit Pistons in which then-Sun Tom Chambers was roughed up:
"They shouldn't hurt Tom Chambers, one of the few white guys who can play. Why don't they hurt white guys who can't play?"
—*Arizona Republic*, 6/25/93

• On then-76er coach Jim Lynam:
"Knute Rockne couldn't make this team win."
—Los Angeles *Times*, 5/3/92

O O O

• On Olympic teammate Karl Malone:
"He's an amazing athlete. He's a bigger me."
—Philadelphia *Inquirer*, 7/23/92

O O O

• On Suns Danny Ainge and Dan Majerle:
"I call them the Ritz twins. They ain't crackers like you all [sportswriters]. You all are saltines. They're strictly Ritz."
—Arizona *Republic*, 6/25/93

O O O

• On whether he'd like to play with his Nike TV commercial sparring partner, Godzilla:
"I've played with enough bad players."
—Arizona *Republic*, 6/25/93

O O O

• On then-Sixer head coach Jim Lynam and then-assistant coach Fred Carter:
"Those guys you can go to war with. You can go out and have a beer with those guys, and if

a guy starts a fight with you, you know you're not by yourself. I respect guys like that a lot."
—*New York Times*, 4/24/89

• On Phoenix Suns teammate Danny Ainge: "People don't know what toughness is. They think it's beating the crud out of people. Well, I can beat the crud out of people if I wanted to, but it's mental toughness. See, Danny Ainge can't beat my mother in basketball, but he's as tough as you can get."
—*New York Times*, 5/27/93

• On why he refers to then-Philadelphia Sixer teammate 6'11" Mark McNamara as "Big Mac": "He used to be able to jump over a Quarter Pounder. He's done some work on his leg. Now he can jump over a Big Mac."
—*Sporting News*, 11/2/87

• Assessing the Sixers:

"There's only two people we can't do without and that's me and Hawk [Hersey Hawkins]. Anybody else we can replace."

—*Sporting News*, 12/10/90

○ ○ ○

• On his role as team leader:

"I try to lead by example. That's my only obligation: to lead by example. I never say anything to someone who is not playing well. I say something to people who are not playing hard. Everybody has a bad game. As long as they play hard, I don't complain."

—Knight-Ridder, 2/4/90

○ ○ ○

• On Sixer owner Harold Katz:

"Harold Katz would rather me be a robot so I can just play and he'll be able to make the money."   —New York *Times*, 11/15/91

○ ○ ○

• On Sixer general manager Gene Shue:

"Gene Shue is a clown whose only ambition in life is to caddie for [Sixer owner] Harold Katz."   —Philadelphia *Daily News*, 6/18/92

• On Dream Teamer John Stockton, who missed four games during the Barcelona Olympics because of a leg injury:
"We call him Chevy Chase. He's over here on a European vacation."
—*Sports Illustrated,* 8/10/92

○ ○ ○

• On the difference between eastern basketball and that in the West:
"Guys thought I was too mean in camp [with the Suns] but they don't get it. You can't just show up on opening night and say, 'OK, now we're going to be mean.' I think living in the sun makes guys soft. John Havlicek told me that. In the East you wake up, you look out and there's snow on the ground. You start the day pissed off. Out here you wake up, it's beautiful out. You put on the Bermudas and have breakfast on the porch."
—*Sports Illustrated,* 11/9/92

○ ○ ○

• On former Sixer shooting guard Andrew Toney:
"I thought he was the best player on the team when I got here. We had Bobby Jones, Moses Malone and Julius Erving but the only one I was in awe of was Andrew."
—Philadelphia *Daily News,* 6/18/92

• After a Sixer practice in 1988:
"We have so many wimps and complainers on this team."

> —Philadelphia *Daily News,* 6/18/92

• On Dan Majerle:
"I thought he was a big country bumpkin, and I was correct. He should be from Alabama. I don't know how he got to Michigan. Majerle is tough. I'd get in a foxhole with him anytime."

> —Minneapolis *Star Tribune,* 6/15/93

• On Detroit general manager Jack McCloskey's comment that the selection of 76er Hersey Hawkins to the All-Star team was a "dark day":
"Hersey deserved to make the team. That's my professional answer. My unprofessional answer is I don't want to hear that bull. If it's a dark day turn your damn lights on."

> —Los Angeles *Times,* 2/11/91

• On the Sixers:

"Am I the reason this team is losing? All I hear about is my bar fights and my book are distracting this team from winning. I've been on the trading block all year, like it's my fault. How about writing an article that says Charles is not the reason that the team is losing; trade some of the other players."

—Washington *Post*, 3/13/92

○ ○ ○
LIFE

• On his daughter, Christiana:
"She's beautiful. Just like her daddy."
                    —Knight-Ridder, 2/4/90

○ ○ ○

• "Stupidity and reality are very close."
                    —New York *Times*, 6/18/90

○ ○ ○

• "I assume people think like I do. That's my
mistake."   —Boston *Globe*, 1/17/92

• On sports in society:
"Sports has really nothing to do with reality."
—*Up Close with Roy Firestone*, ESPN, 2/7/93

○ ○ ○

• On injuring his shoulder during the 1992–93 season:
"Man, the worst thing about this is I won't be able to play golf."
—*Arizona Republic*, 6/25/93

○ ○ ○

• **"Why do bald guys always wear beards? When I started to go bald, I took it like a man."**
—*Arizona Republic*, 6/25/93

○ ○ ○

• On taking up karate:
"I want to be registered as a lethal weapon."
—*Sporting News*, 3/26/90

○ ○ ○

• On the Nike-Reebok controversy, in which the U.S. Olympic Committee insisted all Dream Team members wear Reebok warm-up suits at

the medal ceremony, no matter which company they were signed to represent:
"There are only three things in life that I have to do: I have to stay black, I have to pay taxes and I have to die. Other than that, don't tell me what I have to do."
—St. Louis *Post-Dispatch,* 8/2/92

O O O

• On image:
"Don't judge me by what happens on the court. I'm not a bad guy. There's nobody—nobody—who knows me and doesn't like me."
—*The National,* 4/25/91

O O O

• On his injured back:
"The only time I have fun is when I'm playing, because that's the only time I'm not in pain. The other 22 hours a day I'm in pain all the time." — *The Charlie Rose Show,* 12/3/93

O O O

• On his aspirations to run for governor of Alabama:

"I've accomplished everything pretty much as a rich person. But I think when you get rich, you forget about the less fortunate. And I think our political system is structured like that. Republicans take care of the rich. The Democrats take care of the poor. But I want to be an independent person. If you are in there, you should want to look out for everybody."

—*The Charlie Rose Show,* 12/3/93

○ ○ ○

WINNING

• On whether the Olympics would result in more endorsements:
"I don't need endorsements. All I want is an NBA championship ring and I can live happily ever after." —Boston *Globe*, 8/9/92

• "Unless you win a championship or go deep into the playoffs, I look at the season as a waste. You put nine months of your life into the season. Winning is the only thing that makes it worthwhile."
—New York *Times*, 4/24/89

• On playing with emotion:
"**Emotion is what makes me what I am today. It makes me play bigger than I am.**"
—New York *Times*, 3/17/91

O O O

• After a 1990 win over the New Jersey Nets, with tongue in cheek:
"**This is a game that, if you lose, you go home and beat your wife and kids. Did you see my wife jumping up and down at the end of the game? That's because she knew I wasn't going to beat her.**"   —The *National*, 4/25/91

O O O

• On dissension among the Sixers:
"**Harmony isn't important. The only thing that matters is winning and getting paid.**"
—Los Angeles *Times*, 12/28/89

O O O

• On the 1992 Olympic team:
"**Germans make the best cars and never get bored. Why should Americans get bored when they play the best basketball?**"
—Philadelphia *Inquirer*, 7/23/92

O O O

• "Every time I step onto the court, the guys on the other team are my enemies. The game's not about making friends, it's about winning. As Malcolm X said, 'By any means necessary.' "

—*Outrageous,* p. 204

• After a Game 6 loss to the Chicago Bulls: "I'm *still* going to Disney World."

—Phoenix *Gazette,* 6/24/93

○ ○ ○

LOSING

• After falling behind Chicago 2–0 during the 1993 NBA finals:

"We're in the right state for big holes. Right now we fit right in there with the Grand Canyon." —*Arizona Republic*, 6/25/93

○ ○ ○

• On the Suns losing at Phoenix's AmericaWest Arena for only the second time:

"You're not going to win every game. I'm not the kind to sit around and mope. We started the day with the NBA's best record. We ended the day with the NBA's best record. That's the big picture."

—*Arizona Republic*, 3/1/93

• On never winning an NBA title:

"The only thing I'm guilty of is coming into the league with Larry Bird, Magic Johnson and Michael Jordan."

—*The Charlie Rose Show*, 12/3/93

• On what he was doing in 1972, when the U.S. Olympic men's basketball team suffered a controversial loss to the Soviet Union:

"I had just flunked the entrance exam to kindergarten." —New York *Times*, 7/26/92

○ ○ ○

• On his injured left knee:

"What's the worst that could happen? I could hurt it again and get paid for the next six years. That's not a bad life."

—*Sporting News*, 4/29/91

○ ○ ○

• After losing to the Chicago Bulls in six games in the 1993 NBA finals:
"We live in the desert, it's 90 degrees outside and we can play golf every day. I don't fear losing." —*Arizona Republic,* 6/25/93

○ ○ ○

MONEY

• On the 1988 presidential election when he voted for George Bush:

"My family got all over me because they said Bush is only for the rich people. Then I reminded them, 'Hey, I'm rich.' "

—*Sports Illustrated,* 2/13/89

○ ○ ○

• On whether he would coach sometime down the line just like Paul Westphal is doing after having played for the Suns:

"No, I'll be retired. I'll be a black—oh, I'm sorry—a multimillionaire."

—Minneapolis *Star Tribune,* 6/15/93

• On leading the Sixers in scoring, rebounding and field goal percentage:
"If I'm playing like two people, I want to be paid like two people."

—Chicago Tribune, 12/23/87

○ ○ ○

• "There's no sense in being greedy. I don't want more money than I can spend. My family has everything they need—my mom, my grandmother and my two brothers, my girlfriend and my future kids. I don't need more money. I don't want to die and have $50 million. That's just greedy."

—Los Angeles Times, 2/22/87

○ ○ ○

• "I've enjoyed my eight years in Philadelphia but where I play basketball isn't even one of the 10 most important things in my life. Now that will probably get some people upset. I've got people telling me all the time, 'If you would just go along with the game plan you could be making a couple of million dollars more than you are already.' But what the hell do I need another couple of million for? I'd rather be myself."   —Boston Globe, 1/17/92

• When told by NBA V.P. of operations Rod Thorn that some of the money that the NBA has collected from Barkley in fines would be going to feed needy children:
"Then there can't be a whole lot of hungry kids left in the world."
—*Sporting News,* 11/28/88

O O O

• On being fined $37,000 by the NBA during the 1989–90 season:
"I'll write it off on my income tax."
—*Sports Illustrated,* 7/16/90

O O O

• On whether he could ever return to the 76ers:
"I can be bought. If they paid me enough, I'd work for the Klan."
—*Arizona Republic,* 6/25/93

O O O

• On fines:
"I don't want to go berserk but I saw Jim Courier make an obscene gesture at an official the other night and he got fined $1,000. I'm in the wrong sport. I should take up tennis."
—Minneapolis *Star Tribune,* 1/27/93

• "It's not the crowd or anything that gets me going. I'm thinking about the raise I'm getting after this year. That's what drives me."

—Los Angeles *Times*, 4/9/89

○ ○ ○

• On whether college players should get paid: "Lots of it. Twenty thousand and up. I don't see anything wrong with it. You're providing a service. A lot of schools do it. I thought everybody got paid in college."

—Philadelphia *Daily News*, 10/30/85

○ ○ ○

• On his injured foot during the 1990–91 season:
"In the worst case scenario, I'm out five years and they pay me $16.5 million. In the best case scenario, I play my ass off this year and get a raise."

—Salt Lake City *Tribune*, 2/17/91

○ ○ ○

• On the 1992 All-Star roster:
"Hell, there ain't but 15 black millionaires in the whole country, and half of 'em are right here in this room."

—Minneapolis *Star Tribune*, 6/28/92

• On fines, Rod Thorn and the Pistons:
"I'm convinced that Thorn goes overboard when he fines me, like he's charging me interest. . . . When [my respect] is being challenged, Rod Thorn is the last thing on my mind."

—*Outrageous*, p. 205

○ ○ ○

MEDIA

• On the media horde surrounding him at All-Star Weekends:
"I never realized that you could get so many ugly guys together at the same time."
— *Sporting News*, 3/26/90

• On whether the Nike Air Max's price, $130, is too much for a sportswriter's budget:
"For you guys, $129."
— *Arizona Republic*, 4/12/93

• On his own candor:

"I think I have an obligation to myself and to God to tell the truth. Whether people take it good or bad, that's not my worry. I feel that if you can look yourself in the mirror and honestly feel like you're telling the truth, I think that's all that should matter to you. I think people should say to themselves, 'Is Charles telling the truth?' instead of worrying about who it offends."

—Roy Firestone, *Mouths That Roared*, p. 69

• On whom the media should vote for in 1990 for MVP:

"It just depends on what you guys have been drinking." —*Sporting News*, 3/26/90

• On speaking his mind:

"I believe in expressing what you feel. There are people who hide everything inside—and it's guys like that who kill whole families."

—New York *Times*, 3/17/91

○ ○ ○

• On the Philadelphia media:
"The media doesn't like a strong black athlete who doesn't worry about what's said about him. They're intimidated."

—*Newsday*, 3/10/92

○ ○ ○

• On controversy:
"I don't create controversies. They're there long before I open my mouth. I just bring them to your attention."   —*Outrageous*, p. 37

○ ○ ○

• On his image:
"There's a double standard. If Michael or Magic gets on somebody during a game, people say, 'Oh, look at the leadership he's showing.' If I do it, it's 'There's Charles being immature again.' I'm not trying to be outrageous. But you've got to have controversial figures in sports. You gotta have 'em."

—*Washington Post*, 2/27/91

○ ○ ○

• On being outspoken:
"You can talk without saying a thing. I don't ever want to be that type of person."

—New York *Times*, 3/17/91

O O O

• On what he would do if he retired:
"If push came to shove, I could lose all self-respect and become a reporter."

—*USA Today*, 10/21/93

O O O

○ ○ ○

AFTERWORD

Judge Clarence Thomas once sent me a note that said, "They're going to beat you. Just don't give them the stick to beat you *with*."

Now that you've read all these quotes, you probably see the same thing I see. I've not only given them the stick to beat me with, I've whittled it, shined it up nice and had it Fed-Exed to them. I am constantly amazed how much trouble you can get in just by telling the truth.

The one thing that surprises me most about being a celebrity is how much power your words have. Most black men in this country could go up to city hall and scream at the top of their lungs and people would walk right by them like a hatrack. But I can say one simple little thing, just an innocent remark, and that night it's the lead on ESPN SportsCenter and in every newspaper around the country, and I'm answering questions about it for the next month. All because I can dunk.

It's amazing I haven't given them more sticks. Do you realize how many interviews I do in a week? I remember one time, after I'd answered about the 1000th stupid question of the night from the 1000th ugly reporter of the night. Danny Ainge came up to me and asked, "Don't you ever get tired of it?"

I said, "Hell, yes, I get tired of it. But if I don't do 'em, they'll crucify me." It's true. If you *do* interviews, they love you. If you *don't* do interviews, they kill you. They treat you like Steve Carlton. Or Barry Bonds. Look at Barry Bonds. He is the greatest baseball player of my lifetime, and the press makes him out to be the biggest jerk on the planet. All because he won't give them a decent interview.

I've figured it out. Dealing with the press is like riding a hungry tiger. You'd love to get off, but you have no idea how. If I stopped talking, they'd eat me alive.

So I *have* to keep talking. And as long as I have to keep talking, I at least try to have fun with it so as not to go out of my bald mind.

Writers are always asking me about my regrets. There's two things in life I don't worry about: (1) eating my vegetables and (2) the past. Never. Ever. Everything I did was appropriate for the moment. It might look bad now, but you weren't there *then*, at that *moment*, so you have no right to judge me.

It may look fun to you, but it gets to be a grind being "Charles Barkley" all the time. You have no idea. That's why, when people ask me if I'll miss basketball, I laugh. I'm not going to miss it. I did my time. I'm tired of having people knowing exactly what hotel I'm going to be in on exactly what day. It's like a mouse advertising to a cat when and where, exactly, he's going to be six months a year. That's why, when I retire, I'm going to take up skiing. Who's going to think to look for a large black man on a ski slope? It's all white yuppies and people who speak fluent salmon.

I'm going to sleep late, do what I want, look at my calendar and notice how nice and empty it is. None of this Salt Lake Thursday, Sacramento Friday, Houston Saturday grind. I am going to make a point to schedule in nothing at all about three times a day.

After that I may run for governor of Alabama. And if the yo-yo that's doing it now is any indication, that will be even less work.

—CHARLES BARKLEY

Jordan
is
betteR
than
Barkley